— THE —
WINE-CELLAR
RECORD BOOK

PAVILION
PRODUCTIONS

PAVILION
PRODUCTIONS

First published in 1991 by Pavilion Productions Ltd
A division of Pavilion Books Ltd
196 Shaftesbury Avenue, London WC2H 8JL
Copyright © Pavilion Productions Ltd 1991
Text Copyright © Michael Busselle
Designed by The Third Man
Picture research by Jane Ross
Printed and bound in Italy by L.E.G.O.
ISBN 1 85145 626 0

Acknowledgements

The publishers would like to thank the following for supplying illustrations:

Bridgeman Art Library back cover, pp. 11, 23, 38, 71, 79, 99, 106, 110, 111

Fine Art Photographic front cover, pp. 7, 15, 18, 26, 27, 31, 35, 39, 75, 83, 95, 102, 103, 107

CONTENTS

THE LIFE CYCLE OF WINE

In the simplest terms, wine is a beverage made from fruit juice in a way that creates a degree of alcohol. Why then does it hold such a fascination for so many people? One reason is that it is a living, breathing organism which has a life cycle and character both complex and intriguing – it also has a unique and extremely pleasant flavour!

The process is simple enough. Grape juice contains sugar which is converted by yeasts into alcohol and water. Natural acids and tannin in the skin, pips and stems together with trace elements in the fruit add flavour, bouquet and character.

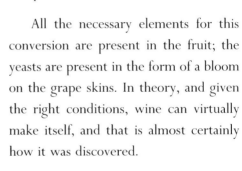

All the necessary elements for this conversion are present in the fruit; the yeasts are present in the form of a bloom on the grape skins. In theory, and given the right conditions, wine can virtually make itself, and that is almost certainly how it was discovered.

In practice, technology lends a hand. The best varieties of grapes are selected to suit the soil and climatic conditions of a particular region. They are pruned and sprayed to raise them to the peak of condition with full ripeness and a high sugar content.

They are harvested when this has been achieved, nominally 100 days after the first appearance of the flowers. In reality this has to be adjusted to allow for factors like lack of sun during the summer months, heavy rains and early and late frosts.

The juice is then extracted by mechanical presses and clarified by centrifuges before being transferred to fermentation vats with carefully controlled temperatures. Additional yeasts are usually added. The complete process of fermentation can take up to several months, during which time the yeasts and sediments sink to the bottom of the vat leaving the wine clear and translucent. Chemicals and pasteurization processes are used to stabilize the wine, and further clarification is achieved by fining and filtration.

At this stage many wines are bottled, but the finer wines are stored in oak casks from periods ranging from a few months to many years in order to mature, developing flavour and character before they are bottled. Further periods of storage in the bottle continue this process.

With the finest wines from single vineyards the use of chemical controls and mechanical processes are kept to an absolute minimum, and the wine is allowed to develop as far as possible in a natural way. It is wines like these which can benefit most from long periods of storage. With such wines the widest variations in quality and character occur with good years and bad years, and they can also display very different characteristics within the same region.

Less expensive wines can be of good quality, but they tend to have a more uniform character and benefit less, if at all, from storing and maturing. Such wines are often made from grapes grown in different vineyards, and very inexpensive wines can result from blending the juice or wines of different regions.

Reading a Label

A wine label is much more than a decorative addition to the bottle: it can be full of very useful information. The most basic fact you can learn is the area in which the wine is produced. With a simple, inexpensive wine like a French *vin du pays* or Spanish *vino de mesa*, for instance, it might simply indicate a very general region like the Loire or Navarra. Other wines will identify a particular part of a wine-growing region, like Bardolino which is produced on the shores of Lake Garda.

The better the wine, the more precise the identification of its origin, to the point where individual villages and vineyards are recorded. If the wine has been bottled at the vineyards or château this too will be recorded, usually both on the label and on the cork, and if it has been imported in bulk and bottled by a shipper or merchant this too is often recorded.

All but the least expensive wines will have the year of the harvest recorded on the label. If this is not present it usually means that the wine has been blended from the product of two or more years' harvests. This happens with even good quality champagnes, because of the way in which they are made.

The alcoholic content is a legally required part of the label. It is becoming common practice to indicate the degree of sweetness or dryness on the label; supermarket wine departments often do this either by description or by a numerical scale, with bone dry at 1 and very sweet at 10. This helps to avoid unhappy purchases when buying an unfamiliar name.

It is becoming quite common now to record the grape types used to make a particular wine, like Chardonnay, Sauvignon or Merlot. This can help to anticipate the characteristics of a wine from an unfamiliar region or country.

An official grading of a wine is also usually recorded on the label. In France, for example, the progression of quality is – starting at the lowest end of the scale – *Vin de Table, Vin du Pays, VDQS, Appellation Controlée* (denoting a general region like Burgundy, for instance) or *Appellation Controlée* (denoting a specific region or village, such as Beaujolais or Fleurie). Other countries have different ways of describing the standard of quality.

Still Life of Apples and Grapes Vincent Clare

Assessing Wine

The quality and character of a particular wine is most easily determined by a sequence of sensory tests. The first is that of appearance. To judge this, a small quantity of wine should be poured into a clear glass with a generous bowl and a narrower rim. It should be tilted so that the surface of the wine creates an ellipse, and is held against a diffused light source. A sheet of well-lit white paper is ideal. In this way the tints of the wine can be seen graded from the shallow area of the meniscus (the curved surface of the liquid) to the full depth of the glass.

You should make an allowance for the nature of light source; a tungsten light bulb, for instance, will make the wine appear more yellow than when seen by daylight, so it is important to try, when possible, to use the same type of illumination for making comparisons.

The colour of white wine can vary from almost white like, say, Frascati, to a light greenish tint like Chablis, or pale straw through to the deep rich golden hue of a Sauternes. As a general rule the depth of colour is an indication of both its alcoholic strength, body, age and sweetness. A deep colour can indicate a full-bodied, well-matured, sweet or strongly alcoholic wine, whereas a pale tint can signal a light, dry, young wine.

With reds the colour can range from a pale, almost rose-like tint like a Spanish *clarete*, for example, to a clear bright open colour and a deep purple or brown tinge. The latter is usually an indication of a well-matured

wine, and indicative of oak-cask storage. Rosé wines can also show a wide range of colour from the deep tint of an Arbois to the off-white pinkness of, for example, a Vin Gris.

The country or region of origin can also be reflected in the colour of a wine. Wines from hot climates like Australia tend to have an inherently deeper colour compared to wines from cooler climes. A Californian Chardonnay, for example, would be much drier than, say, a Moselle, although the former might have a deeper colour.

The second test is that of bouquet or aroma. This is harder to identify and certainly to describe. The aroma of wine is usually most prominent when first poured from the bottle, and can be accentuated by swirling lightly around the glass. Your nose should be thrust well into the glass to inhale deeply but normally. An experienced wine buyer can tell a great deal about the taste of a wine from its bouquet alone. The presence of excess tannin or acidity and lack of fullness or body can soon be judged with experience.

The vocabulary for describing the flavours and aromas of wines is often very personal, and may not mean much to another person unless the same references are used. References to fruit flavours are common, like blackcurrants or strawberries, for instance, but with aromas you will often hear more eccentric descriptions. Recently I heard bananas and bubble gum attributed to a white wine.

It is not at all uncommon for very young or inexpensive wines to have little or no aroma. This doesn't mean they will have no taste, but rather that they are likely to lack body and character; they may well be perfectly drinkable on a less critical level.

Tasting a wine requires a little ceremony. Normal drinking habits often result in a wine not receiving full critical attention. A small quantity should be taken into the mouth and moved around so that it makes contact with all parts of the tongue, since different taste buds detect different aspects of the flavour.

It helps to take in some air with the wine: experienced tasters swish the wine back and forth between their teeth. In this way both aroma and taste can be sensed together. When several wines are to be tasted it is common practice to spit each out between samples. Those less experienced in tasting, however, will probably be able to make a more positive judgement by swallowing it.

The qualities to look for when tasting, and smelling, are the degree of acidity, the strength of the tannin, the relative sweetness and dryness of

the wine and the existence of an aftertaste when it has been swallowed or ejected. An excess of chemical stabilizers is often most easily detected at this stage, and the taste of fine wine will linger pleasurably for some time. Such chemical tastes are sometimes masked by wine makers by the use of greater acidity and sweetness, so this too is something to look for. Good wines have a more complex taste and aroma which can take longer to assimilate and assess compared to a simple inexpensive wine.

For obvious reasons tasting should take place in an environment which is as neutral as possible; cigarette smoke, aftershave or scent are not recommended, and it helps to clear the palate before and between samples by eating a dry biscuit or a piece of bread.

VINTAGE CHART

Bordeaux (Médoc/Graves)	1900, 1928, 1929, 1945, 1949, 1953, 1961, 1966, 1970, 1975, 1978, 1982, 1985, 1986
Bordeaux (St.-Emilion/Pomerol)	1900, 1928, 1929, 1945, 1949, 1953, 1961, 1966, 1975, 1982, 1985
Bordeaux (Sauternes/Barsac)	1937, 1945, 1947, 1949, 1955, 1959, 1962, 1975, 1983, 1986
Burgundy (Côte d'Or – Red)	1915, 1919, 1929, 1945, 1949, 1959, 1961, 1969, 1971, 1985
Burgundy (Côte d'Or – White)	1921, 1928, 1962, 1964, 1969, 1985, 1986
Burgundy (Beaujolais – Red)	1929, 1945, 1949, 1957, 1959, 1961, 1976, 1978, 1983, 1985
Champagne	1914, 1921, 1928, 1945, 1947, 1959, 1964, 1966, 1969, 1970, 1979, 1981, 1983
Alsace	1921, 1937, 1945, 1949, 1953, 1959, 1961, 1966, 1969, 1971, 1975, 1983, 1985
Loire (Sweet White)	1921, 1945, 1949, 1959, 1961, 1969, 1971, 1975, 1976, 1983
Loire (Red)	1961, 1969, 1975, 1976, 1985
Rhône (Northern Rhône – Red)	1961, 1964, 1970, 1972, 1978, 1982, 1983, 1985
Rhône (Southern Rhône – Red)	1961, 1964, 1967, 1970, 1972, 1978, 1983, 1985
Germany (Mosel-Saar-Ruwer)	1921, 1945, 1949, 1953, 1959, 1964, 1969, 1971, 1973, 1975, 1976, 1983, 1985, 1986
Germany (Rhine)	1921, 1945, 1949, 1953, 1959, 1964, 1969, 1971, 1975, 1976, 1983, 1985, 1986

This chart lists the years from the beginning of the twentieth century which are generally considered to have produced the best wines in a particular category. Like all vintage charts, it does not pretend to be a foolproof guide, and wines within a category will vary from region to region and vineyard to vineyard, but it is worth making a note of the years which have consistently produced wines of a high quality.

Italy (Barolo)	1922, 1931, 1947, 1958, 1964, 1971, 1978, 1982, 1983, 1985
Italy (Chianti)	1911, 1928, 1931, 1947, 1971, 1982, 1985
Spain (Rioja)	1916, 1920, 1924, 1934, 1942, 1962, 1964, 1968, 1970, 1982, 1983
Portugal (Vintage Port)	1908, 1927, 1931, 1935, 1945, 1963, 1967, 1970, 1977, 1983, 1985
USA (California – Red)	1946, 1951, 1964, 1968, 1970, 1974, 1983, 1984, 1985, 1987
USA (California – White)	1964, 1967, 1970, 1974, 1980, 1984, 1987
USA (Pacific Northwest – Red)	1975, 1983, 1985
USA (Pacific Northwest – White)	1983, 1985, 1986
Australia (Hunter Valley – Red)	1965, 1975, 1979, 1980, 1983, 1985, 1986
Australia (Hunter Valley – White)	1967, 1979, 1980, 1983, 1985, 1986, 1987
Australia (Barossa Valley – Red)	1976, 1979, 1982, 1984, 1985
Australia (Barossa Valley – White)	1976, 1978, 1979, 1982, 1984, 1985, 1986
Australia (Margaret River – Red)	1977, 1982, 1985
Australia (Margaret River – White)	1980, 1982, 1985

CLASSIC GRAPE TYPES

The variety of grape used to make wine has an enormous effect on its quality and character. The permutations which are possible from the basic grape varieties combined with hybrids, the soil, climate, blends and methods of production are some of the factors which make wine such a complex and fascinating subject.

There is a nucleus, however, of grape varieties from which the best-known and most influential styles of wine are produced, and an understanding of these is a valuable aid to tasting and assessing wines.

CABERNET SAUVIGNON

Of the black grapes from which red wines are produced the Cabernet Sauvignon is the one with perhaps the widest international popularity. It is thought to have derived from wild vines first grown in the Bordeaux area of France and remains the foundation of the red wines of that region. It is also grown widely throughout Europe as well as North and South America, Australia, Africa and New Zealand.

The small, almost sloelike, purple berries ripen late and contain generous tannin, due in part to an abundance of pips and a high proportion of pulp to juice when pressed. Although initially harsh or tough in character this grape makes a wine destined to keep and mature. Its bouquet is one of blackcurrant fruit and when aged has a fat buttery taste with masses of body and flavour.

The Cabernet Franc, also widely grown in Bordeaux, has a softer taste with more complex aroma. It is commonly used as a component of clarets and also in red wines from the Loire, like Saumur Champigny.

MERLOT

This too is an important high-yield grape variety grown extensively in south-west France and used as a blend for Medoc, St Emilion and Graves. It is used less frequently in France as a single-grape wine, but is popular in Italy and Eastern Europe. Rare in Spain, it is, however, used in the country's most renowned wine, Vega Sicilia. It is valued for its fruitiness but lacks tannin and acid, making it an ideal partner for the Cabernet Sauvignon.

PINOT NOIR

The great red-wine grape of Burgundy is more fickle and less easily identifiable than the Cabernet Sauvignon and not as widely grown elsewhere in the world. It is, however, grown in Alsace, the Savoie and Jura and is an essential ingredient of most champagnes where it is pressed swiftly to produce a colourless juice. It is also grown in Germany, northern Italy, Hungary and California.

A low-yield grape, it produces a wine with flavours of red fruits and can mature to create highly complex tastes and bouquets with an excellent finish and considerable potential to improve with age.

SYRAH

This is the grape which gives many of the red Rhône wines, like Hermitage, their great strength and character. It accounts for a relatively small proportion of French red wines but is grown widely in Australia as Shiraz. It survives well on poor soil with a fair yield and has an abundance of tannin, producing strongly alcoholic wines with plenty of body and flavour and the potential for high quality and improvement with keeping.

GAMAY

Beaujolais is a wine and a region where the Gamay reigns supreme. It accounts for a high proportion of French red wines and is characteristic of the young fresh reds which constitute the great fount of everyday wine.

The Gamay produces a light purple-tinged red wine with good fruit, acidity and bouquet but relatively low in tannin and, consequently, best drunk young. It has a high yield and lends itself well to the rapid vinification which has helped to make the Beaujolais Nouveau such a marketing success.

It is used as a blend with Pinot Noir in Burgundy's Passe-Tout-Grains and also flourishes in the Loire, Savoie and Jura, but is seldom found in other parts of the world.

CHARDONNAY

The Chardonnay is probably the most popular and widely planted white-wine grape the world over. From California and South Africa to Bulgaria and Italy to Australia it is one of the most favoured vines and is relatively easy to grow with a good yield. In France it is, arguably, *the* grape from which the classic Burgundies, like Montrachet and Chablis, are made. It is also used to make Blanc des Blancs Champagne.

It produces a delicately flavoured, full-bodied wine with a good balance of acidity and alcohol together with a fragrant aroma. It also has great potential to improve with age.

SAUVIGNON BLANC

This grape produces the other great French white wines of Sancerre and Pouilly Fumé as well as being an important element in the white wines of Graves where it is blended with Semillon. It is widely grown in other regions of France like the Touraine and Poitou as well as northern Italy, California, South Africa and Australia.

It produces a light fresh wine with a hint of green fruit in the bouquet and a flinty-dry flavour, but has a limited potential to improve.

CHENIN BLANC

Grown widely in the Loire valley, where it is used to make wines like Vouvray and Côteaux de Layon, the Chenin Blanc, or Pineau de la Loire, is found in most wine-growing countries. A high-yielding grape, it produces

a wine which can make both sweet honeyed wines and those which are bone dry with equal success. Its bouquet is often associated with citrus fruits like quince and lime with hints of honey.

As well as making both sweet and dry wines the Chenin Blanc is also used to make sparkling wines. Outside France it is popular in the United States, South Africa and Australia.

COLOMBARD

This is the grape from which much of the Armagnac and Cognac production is distilled. It is used as a blend for many types of white wine

A Tribute to Bacchus Jean-Baptiste Robie

but in the Côtes de Blaye is used to make a single-grape wine as it is in Gascony, South Africa, South America and Australia.

It makes light fresh wines with a good bouquet and balance but is not a wine for keeping and is best drunk young.

RIESLING

As universal as the Chardonnay, the Riesling grape originated in Germany along the banks of the Rhine. It is widely grown in Alsace, Hungary, Yugoslavia, the United States, South Africa and Australia. It is a high-yielding grape which, like the Semillon, when harvested late is susceptible to noble rot, enabling both sweet and dry wines to be made.

With a good balance of acidity and alcohol it makes wines that are aromatic, fresh and clean-tasting with considerable potential to improve with age.

SEMILLON

Widely grown in south-west France, the Semillon grape is used as a component of dry white wines in combination with Sauvignon Blanc. It is also ideal for the generation of *botrytis cinera*, the noble rot from which a highly concentrated juice is pressed to make sweet white wines like Sauternes.

It produces a strongly alcoholic wine, relatively low in acidity and with a limited bouquet, having what is usually described as a grassy, lemony flavour. Outside France it is grown in Australia, particularly in Hunter's Valley where it is used to make a single-grape wine, as well as in combination with Chardonnay. It is also popular in eastern Europe, South Africa and California.

BUYING WINE

Buying wine can, and should be, a great source of pleasure. While browsing along the racks of a good supplier you have, at your fingertips, an immense variety of choice. The country or region of origin, the skills of individual wine-makers, the characteristics of specific vineyards and grape types, the benevolence, or otherwise, of the climate and weather conditions during a particular year and the fascinating, and sometimes unpredictable, effects of the passage of time. Such a choice is, on one hand, exciting and on the other rather daunting, especially if there is the possibility of expensive errors.

If you are buying very expensive fine wines or *primeurs* with the intention of perhaps investment, or to build a cellar for decades to come, then, unless you are an expert, the knowledge, experience and advice of a reliable and unbiased wine merchant is essential. Such merchants often hold periodic tastings for regular clients which allow you to explore new possibilities at little or no cost.

Off-licences and supermarkets can offer good value and reliability on a more modest level, and the choice can sometimes be exceptional. The wine magazines have frequent lists of newly available products and tasting notes which can enable you to do some armchair selection for a potential shopping list.

Tasting a wine in such places is rarely possible and the best method is to simply buy a selection of single bottles in which you are interested to try at home. This method, in any case, can be easier for the less experienced when making assessments in a more relaxed and leisurely way. After you have made your choice, if you order by the case, or in excess of a certain value, many such retailers will offer good discounts.

Perhaps the most enjoyable way of buying wine is at its source from a vineyard. In some cases there is not necessarily much saving in cost, especially with finer, more highly priced wines. I have seen English supermarket prices below that of the same bottle from a French vineyard. It can be great fun, however, to visit a few vineyards and import your own wines on a modest scale. An enquiry at the local customs and excise office will reveal the current allowance for duty and tax when estimating the total cost if you intend to exceed the normal allowance.

Although at the very top vineyards it is necessary to make appointments, or have professional connections, the situation at smaller enterprises can be very formal. Most vineyards, if they sense you are seriously interested in buying, will freely offer a tasting.

In addition to individual wine-makers, the *cave* co-operatives can offer a good blend of value and quality. Don't ignore the roadside *caveaux*, these are often a useful and convenient way of introducing yourself to the wines of regions through which you are passing. A list of vineyards and *cave* co-operatives can be obtained from both national and local tourist offices as well as from organisations like *Food and Wine of France*.

When eating out in local restaurants, a study of the wine list will usually reveal a few useful names and addresses and the opportunity to do some preliminary tasting. A good restaurant can also be the source of sound advice concerning suppliers.

Wine-dealer.

For more casual, everyday wines it is also possible to buy wine in bulk – *en vrac* – in large plastic containers holding five litres or more. This method of storage is quite satisfactory for short periods but it can be decanted into clean sterilised bottles at home for longer keeping. Buying wine in this way can offer considerable savings over exactly the same wine in bottles.

It is also worth seeking out wine fairs and festivals, of which there are thousands, when travelling through wine-growing regions, since these are both a great deal of fun and a way of tasting, usually quite free, the products of several individual wine-growers at the same place.

Another satisfying and enjoyable way of buying good-quality wines at relatively low cost is to explore the possibilities afforded by the less well-known and widely exported wine regions. In France, for instance, the wines of St Pourcin-sur-Sioule or Quincy offer lower-priced alternatives to

Sancerre or Pouilly Fumé. Off-the-beaten track vineyards like the Côtes des Toul or Marcillac, for example, tend to have a better price and quality ratio than some of the more popular wine regions. A collection of such wines can have the added pleasure of rarity value since many are unavailable, or hard to find, outside the region of production.

Take care to pack your wine so that it is subjected to the least possible disturbance when travelling and try to avoid leaving it, say, in a car boot, in places where the temperature is likely to soar or plummet to extremes.

The Favourite Cesare-Auguste Detti

SERVING WINE

Wine deserves a little ceremony even if it is a simple *vin du pays*. Much of the pleasure of wine is visual, and a good glass is the starting point for the anticipated delights to follow. There are different types of glass for different wines, but the main criterion is a clean simple shape and clear untinted glass to allow the colour to be seen.

It should have a stem, which enables the warmth of the hand to be isolated from the wine, a good base for stability and a rim which is narrower than the width of the bowl. This helps to concentrate and contain the bouquet, although champagne flutes sometimes breach this rule in order to allow the full release of the bubbles.

The bottle should also be treated with respect. A young wine can be carried and placed on to the table (covered with a plain white cloth to show the colour) in an upright position beside the waiting glasses. An older wine with sediment should be held in a basket at a similar angle to the wine rack in order to keep the sediment at the base of the bottle.

Even pulling the cork can be an enjoyable aspect of the wine and a good corkscrew is an asset to the wine lover. The waiter's friend – pocketknife style with a blade for removing the capsule and a lever to assist the pull – has all the traditional charm but the more modern screwpull is perhaps easier to use and still creates a nice sensation as the cork comes out. When the cork is removed it should be sniffed to ensure there is no contamination, and the bottle neck wiped clean. A small amount of wine can then be poured into a glass to be swirled, sniffed and tasted as a final check before serving.

It is claimed that some wines benefit from being uncorked several hours before serving, this can help to clear any unpleasant odours caused by stabilisation, storage or ageing and to help release the bouquet. Some experts, however, assert that 'letting a wine breath' has no significant effect after the first few minutes. An old wine with sediment should be carefully decanted to ensure that the sediment is left behind in the bottle.

Temperature too is a vital consideration. As a general rule, temperature is coupled to body. A light wine, whether white, rosé or red, is best served at a significantly lower temperature than a full-bodied wine. White wines should normally be served at the lower end of the temperature scale.

Chambre, or room temperature, means little for reds any more since the advent of the higher ambient temperatures created by central heating. As a general rule, the recommended cellar temperature range of 10 to 16 degrees Celsius is a good guide. A cheap thin white, or sweet white dessert wine, can benefit from being a degree or so lower, and a particularly full-bodied or well-matured red wine can benefit from being a degree or two higher. Ultimately, however, it is personal taste, the circumstances and the accompanying food which should dictate.

When the moment arrives to serve the wine it should be poured slowly and smoothly into the glass to somewhere between half and two-thirds full – never close to the rim.

STORING WINE

A suitable place to keep wine is an essential prerequisite of buying a long-term stock. It makes little sense to invest large sums of money if there is a risk of the wine deteriorating before you can drink it. This is, of course, especially true of fine wines where good storage conditions can actually contribute to the development and improvement of the wine.

It is well to consider the reasons for storing wine. They usually fall into several categories. There are wines for everyday drinking where the convenience of a ready and accessible supply is the main concern. In this case the turnover is likely to be quite swift and the storage conditions can

be less critical. A rack in a cool dark corner of the house could be both quite suitable as well as easy to get at.

The next category is for rather better wines, those selected for special occasions and dinner parties where they are ready to drink but perhaps kept for a year or so, and the main concern is to avoid deterioration.

For wines where the intention is to keep it for very long periods, say five years or more, the closer you can meet the ideal conditions afforded by a wine cellar the better. Some wine merchants offer cellarage facilities to clients who are buying for long-term investment and wines which are not intended to be drunk in the foreseeable future, and this can be a better option for those who lack the right facilities themselves.

Even for periods of one to five years it is still necessary to be quite careful about temperature and humidity. Although a cellar is traditionally the place where wines are kept, a below-ground storage space is not obligatory. Many fine wines are kept in *chais* (wine store-houses), or above-ground storage places and, in any case, a cellar which is not designed for wine storage may well be less suitable than a cupboard or outhouse with the right conditions of temperature and humidity.

The main criteria is that the area in which the wines are stored should be free from vibration and odours with little or no daylight. The temperature should not drop below about ten degrees Celsius or rise above sixteen, and the relative humidity is best at between sixty and ninety degrees.

There is no need for all your wines to be kept in the same place. Smaller insulated, temperature-controlled areas can be used for your very best wines. It is possible to buy special cupboards for this purpose and it is also feasible to use an old, disconnected, chest freezer. You might even consider digging a small cellar in a convenient spot in an outhouse or below a garage, for instance.

Wine bottles should be stored on their sides so that the liquid is in contact with the corks, which prevents the risk of air leaking into the bottle should the cork dry out and shrink. They should slope slightly with the neck uppermost so that any sediment formed will sink slowly to the base of the bottle. Simple metal and wood wine racks designed to hold the bottles in the right position are readily available in units of a dozen or more and can be stacked easily in convenient configurations and fixed to the wall for stability.

Wine bought in bulk, in plastic containers or barrels, for instance, should be bottled before storage unless the entire contents are likely to be used within a short period of time – for a party perhaps. Bottling is easy and the essentials can be bought at a good home wine-making supplier. Bottles must be thoroughly cleaned and sterilised and the wine siphoned carefully down the sides so that no froth and subsequent oxidation is caused.

Corks should also be sterilised and soaked in hot water to soften them, before driving fully into the bottle neck so that only a small space exists between the end of the cork and the surface of the wine. A simple wooden corking device can be bought inexpensively. The cork and bottle top should then be covered with a plastic or metal-foil capsule and the bottle labelled. If you buy your bulk wine from a vineyard or co-operative they will usually be able to supply you with labels.

MAKING TASTING NOTES

One of the main functions of this book is to provide a record of the wines you have tasted and your impressions of them. It is surprising how quickly it is possible to forget or confuse the judgements you make, and brief notes should be recorded between each sample.

Since these records are primarily for your own personal use it does not matter too much what words you use to describe the various qualities, as long as you use the same terms in similar instances. A description like 'fuchsia' is fine, providing you have an accurate image in your mind of the colour this means to you in terms of density and hue.

Bouquet is more complex to describe, and the best way is to get to know the aromas of the basic grape types and to have a readily understandable description for each. If you think that a Beaujolais smells like rhubarb and custard, then the next time you smell a wine made from the Gamay grape you will have a good point of reference with which to compare. It can also help to establish a scale for the dominant aromas. A scale of 1 to 10, for instance, can be used for acidity, tannin and fruit.

Taste is easier to describe than bouquet but still tends to rely on fairly subjective associations, although there is a more widely accepted common vocabulary for flavours. Again, establishing a scale for sweetness, fruit and body is helpful, so too is a clear flavour reference for the basic grape types.

You also need to make a summary of your impressions and prognosis. An excess of acidity and tannin in a young wine, for example, is something which can often correct itself with greater maturity. It might be noted that a white wine which is showing a deepening of colour, or a red which has a brownish tinge, should not be kept much longer.

It is important to record the date of each tasting and, if accompanied by food, it can help to record the dishes which were served and whether they were compatible. Full label information should also, of course, be recorded, together with the source of supply for future reference.

WINE AND FOOD

Some would claim that wine and food are a partnership made in heaven and celebrated in paradise. Maybe going too far, but a good meal accompanied by a fine wine is, for many, one of life's better experiences.

Serious wine-drinkers will go as far as making the choice of wine the predominant consideration and the food relegated to a mere supporting role. For most, however, a happy balance which enhances each is the main aim.

The old-fashioned, simplistic rule of red wine with meat and white with fish does have a core of good sense in that a light fruity wine with a degree of acidity suits a subtly flavoured food best, while a full-bodied wine with a tannic toughness makes a better companion for a strongly flavoured dish.

In practice a lightly chilled Beaujolais, like a Chiroubles, can make an ideal partner to some fish dishes, while a full-bodied rich Chardonnay could combine well with a well-sauced veal dish or roasted pork, for instance. And while you might choose a good strong red like a Spanish Ribera del Duero to accompany *rillettes d'oie*, or a coarse *pâté de campagne*, a sweet white wine like Sauternes is commonly served with *pâté de foie gras*.

It is not necessarily the main ingredient which should dictate the choice of wine, since flavourings and sauces can often dominate a dish. Although a white wine would be a suitable accompaniment to say a *fricassée de volaille*, a full-bodied red would be the choice for the classic *coq au vin*.

It is rather unfashionable, but if you are in doubt about a choice of red or white to accompany a dish a good rosé might well solve the problem, a Les Riceyes or Tavel, for instance, or a blush Zinfandel.

Be cautious of serving food that is significantly acidic, such as dishes with a vinaigrette dressing, since this can destroy the taste of even the best wines. Some acidic vegetable dishes like spinach or even tomatoes can also create problems in the same way, although in Alsace the Riesling or Gewurztraminer is drunk enthusiastically with the local acidic speciality of *choucroute*.

Highly spiced foods too can be a problem; the classic dilemma of what to drink with curry is a good example. Well-chilled slightly acidic white wines can be a solution to some of these cases. These are circumstances, however, where it can make good sense to temper the choice of food to avoid clashes or compromises with the wine.

As a general rule it is best, if a variety of wines are to be served with a meal, to start with white or lighter wines and progress to reds and more full-bodied wines.

Red wine is usually the choice for cheese, but there can be exceptions. The Alsace Munster, flavoured with cumin seeds, is traditionally served with the spicy Gewurztraminer and the pungent Crottin de Chavignol demands a glass of Sancerre.

THE LANGUAGE OF WINE

ACIDITY A necessary element in wine and a natural component of grape juice. It gives a wine crispness and freshness. An excess can create a harsh abrasive character and too little can make a wine taste flat.

AFTERTASTE When a wine has been swallowed it often leaves a lingering flavour on the palate. An unpleasant aftertaste can be the result of excessive use of chemicals or poor storage. A pleasant aftertaste which continues to develop in complexity is a characteristic of a fine wine which is then described as having a good finish.

ALCOHOL A vital ingredient in most wines and the result of the fermentation of the sugar in grape juice. As a general rule, a wine with a high degree of alcohol is full-bodied and is more likely to improve with keeping. A low degree of alcohol results in a light, even thin, wine which will be best drunk young.

Most table wines have a level of between 10 and 15 degrees of alcohol. Much more than this halts the process of fermentation, and strongly alcoholic ('fortified') wines like sherry and port are created by adding distilled grape spirit to naturally fermented wine.

Inexpensive wines like French *vin de table* sometimes have a lower degree of alcohol, so too do wines from regions with climates which do not allow the grapes to ripen to a full sugar content, like some English and German wines.

AUSTERE A wine which lacks body and flavour.

BALANCE The reaction and degree of harmony between the various elements of flavour inherent in a wine. A well-balanced wine has acidity, fruit, tannin, body and a degree of alcohol which have combined to create a taste in which no one element dominates to excess. It could also be described as well-rounded.

BLANC DE BLANCS A white wine made from only white grapes, such as Chardonnay or Chenin Blanc.

BLANC DE NOIRS A white wine made by pressing black grapes quickly so that the juice is not allowed to take colour from the pigments in the skins. Most champagne, for example, is made from a blend of the juice of one variety of white grapes and two types of black grapes.

CARBONIC MACERATION A process in which the grapes are macerated before fermentation in order to reduce the period needed before bottling, as in the case of Nouveaux wines.

CAPSULE The small sleeve which is fitted over the cork. Plastic is now commonly used, but fine wines are still sealed with lead or foil capsules.

CAVE A below ground-level storage space for wines.

CAVE CO-OPERATIVE A wine-making establishment where individual growers bring their grapes for the entire production process to be carried out and marketed in larger and more economic quantities than would be possible for them as independent wine-makers.

CÉPAGE The French word for the grape variety.

CHAIS An above-ground storage area for wine.

CHAPTALISATION The technique of adding sugar to grape juice when the sugar content is too low to ensure the required degree of alcohol.

CLOSED A wine which has little or no bouquet and lacks flavour.

COUPAGE The technique of blending wines of different origins and an essential process in the production of most champagnes.

CREMANT A sparkling wine which has a lower degree of effervescence than normal.

DECANTING The process of pouring the contents of a wine bottle into a jug in order to separate it from sediment which has collected at the base of the bottle. It is usually only necessary with fine, well-matured wines.

DRY A wine which has little or no residual sugar after fermentation.

FINISH The aftertaste which lingers on the palate when the wine has been swallowed. A good, lasting and complex aftertaste is the mark of a fine wine.

FLABBY A term used to describe a wine which lacks the acidity and tannin necessary to give it freshness and flavour.

FORTIFIED A wine with distilled grape spirit added to increase its degree of alcohol, such as port, sherry or madeira.

KIR A popular French aperitif made, in its correct form, by adding a small quantity of cassis to a white Burgundy made from the Aligote grape. It takes its name from a former mayor of Lyon.

Man with a Glass of Wine Portuguese School

PASTEURISATION A process of stabilisation where the wine is heated to a temperature which destroys the active bacteria remaining after fermentation is complete.

PÉTILLANT A wine which has very slight amount of effervescence.

PHYLLOXERA An aphid which destroys vines. It wiped out vast areas of the European vineyards in the middle of the nineteenth century and was only controlled by grafting new vines on to aphid-resistant American root stocks.

LIQUOREUX A sweet wine with a high degree of alcohol.

LONG A wine which has a pronounced and lingering aftertaste.

MADERISED A wine which has discoloured through excessive ageing and oxidation.

MARC The residue of skins, pips and stems left after the grapes are pressed. It is boiled up and distilled to make *eau de vie*.

MÉTHODE CHAMPENOISE The process by which sparkling wines are produced in which a controlled secondary fermentation takes place after bottling.

MILLESIMÉ The French word to describe a wine produced from a specific vineyard in a good year.

MOELLEUX A term used to describe a smooth, well-rounded, luscious wine.

MOUSSEUX A sparkling wine.

MUST The fermenting grapes after they have been crushed.

NEGOÇIANT A wine-merchant or broker who is also involved with the production of the wine he sells in co-operation with the wine-growers who supply him. A common practice in Burgundy.

NOBLE ROT The mould which develops on the skin of grapes which have been left on the vines after ripening. It creates a highly concentrated, sugary juice from which sweet white dessert wines, like Sauternes, Bergerac or Barsac, are made.

NOUVEAU A wine which has been vinified in a way which enables it to be bottled, and drunk, within a few weeks of fermentation.

OAKY A taste influenced by the oak cask in which a wine was matured.

OXIDATION The effect on wine of excessive ageing or exposure to air, through a defective cork for example, which results in red wines taking on a brownish tinge and white wines deepening in colour.

SPRITZIG The German term for describing wines with a very slight degree of effervescence and the origin of name given to a mixture of white wine and mineral water – spritzer.

STALKY A wine which has an excess of tannin, possibly as a result of leaving the juice for too long in contact with the must after pressing.

SUPPLE A favourite term used to describe a well-rounded wine with a good balance of acidity and tannin.

TOUGH A full-bodied wine exhibiting an excess of tannin, and which is expected to improve and mellow with age.

VIN DE GARDE A wine to keep and one which is expected to improve.

VINIFICATION The process of converting grapes into wine.

VINTAGE A wine made from the grapes from a specific year's harvest.

CELLAR RECORDS

Date Purchased	Wine	Supplier	Price	Date and No. of bottles used

Comments	Remaining stock

Date Purchased	Wine	Supplier	Price	Date and No. of bottles used

Comments	Remaining stock

Date Purchased	Wine	Supplier	Price	Date and No. of bottles used

Comments	Remaining stock

Date Purchased	Wine	Supplier	Price	Date and No. of bottles used

Comments	Remaining stock

Date Purchased	Wine	Supplier	Price	Date and No. of bottles used

Comments	Remaining stock

Date Purchased	Wine	Supplier	Price	Date and No. of bottles used

Comments	Remaining stock

Date Purchased	Wine	Supplier	Price	Date and No. of bottles used

Comments	Remaining stock

Date Purchased	Wine	Supplier	Price	Date and No. of bottles used

Comments	Remaining stock

Date Purchased	Wine	Supplier	Price	Date and No. of bottles used

Comments	Remaining stock

Date Purchased	Wine	Supplier	Price	Date and No. of bottles used

Comments	Remaining stock

Date Purchased	Wine	Supplier	Price	Date and No. of bottles used

Comments	Remaining stock

Date Purchased	Wine	Supplier	Price	Date and No. of bottles used

Comments	Remaining stock

Date Purchased	Wine	Supplier	Price	Date and No. of bottles used

Comments	Remaining stock

Date Purchased	Wine	Supplier	Price	Date and No. of bottles used

Comments	Remaining stock

DISCOVERIES

Date	Wine	Where Tasted	Price	Comments	Source

Date	Wine	Where Tasted	Price	Comments	Source

The Stirrup Cup Eugen Joseph Verboeckhoven

Date	Wine	Where Tasted	Price	Comments	Source

Date	Wine	Where Tasted	Price	Comments	Source

Date	Wine	Where Tasted	Price	Comments	Source

Date	Wine	Where Tasted	Price	Comments	Source

Date	Wine	Where Tasted	Price	Comments	Source

Date	Wine	Where Tasted	Price	Comments	Source

Date	Wine	Where Tasted	Price	Comments	Source

Date	Wine	Where Tasted	Price	Comments	Source

Portrait of a Man Holding a Glass of Wine Jan van Bylert

Date	Wine	Where Tasted	Price	Comments	Source

Date	Wine	Where Tasted	Price	Comments	Source

Date	Wine	Where Tasted	Price	Comments	Source

Date	Wine	Where Tasted	Price	Comments	Source

The Grape Harvest Anon.

LABEL SCRAPBOOK

84

CHIROUBLES

Mosel · Saar · Ruwer

LAIS-VILLAGES

MÉTHODE CHAMPENOISE

Varichon & Clerc

VIN MOUSSEUX

BLANC DE BLANCS

RIESLING SPÄTLESE

1986er EITELSBACHER KARTH

750 ml

JULES ROBIN

PINEAU DES CHARENTES

Bunan

VIN DE PAYS DU MONT CAUME

CABERNET SAUVIGNON

1985

BANDOL

APPELLATION BANDOL CONTRÔLÉE

MAS de la ROUVIÈRE

1985

BUNAN VIGNERON AU CASTELLET VAR

MIS EN BOUTEILLE À LA PROPRIÉTÉ

PRODUCE OF FRANCE

87

RIESLING SPÄTLESE

1986er EITELSBACHER KARTH
750 ml

VOSNE-ROMANÉE
LES MALCONSORTS
APPELLATION CONTRÔLÉE

Domaine du Clos Frantin
PROPRIÉTAIRE À VOSNE-ROMANÉE, CÔTE-D'OR

70cl

JULES
ROBIN

PINEAU
DES
CHARENTES

FRANCE

Bunan
VIN DE PAYS DU
MONT CAUME

CABERNET
SAUVIGNON

1985

BANDOL
APPELLATION BANDOL CONTRÔLÉE

MAS de la ROUVIÈRE
1985

BUNAN VIGNERON AU CASTELLET VAR

PRODUCE OF FRANCE

RIESLING SPÄTLESE

1986er EITELSBACHER KARTH

750 ml

VOSNE·ROMANÉE
LES·MALCONSORTS

Domaine du Clos Frantin

PROPRIÉTAIRE À VOSNE-ROMANÉE, CÔTE-D'OR

70cl · 17%vol

JULES
ROBIN

PINEAU
DES
CHARENTES

FRANCE

Bunan

VIN DE PAYS DU
MONT CAUME

CABERNET
SAUVIGNON

1985

BANDOL
APPELLATION BANDOL CONTRÔLÉE

MAS de la ROUVIÈRE
1985

MÉDAILLE D'ARGENT · PARIS 1986

BUNAN VIGNERON AU CASTELLET VAR
MIS EN BOUTEILLE À LA PROPRIÉTÉ

PRODUCE OF FRANCE

CHATEAU
LYNCH & BAGES
GRAND CRU CLASSÉ
PAUILLAC

CHIROUBLES
APPELLATION CHIROUBLES CONTRÔLÉE

Mosel · Saar · Ruwer
1983 Serriger Vogelsang
Riesling Eiswein
375 ml

OLAIS-VILLAGES

NE PEDAUQUE

MÉTHODE CHAMPENOISE
MÉTHODE TRADITIONNELLE

PRODUCT OF FRANCE

Varichon & Clerc
VIN MOUSSEUX
750 ml   11.5% vol

BLANC DE BLANCS

MEALS TO REMEMBER

Date	Place And Occasion	Food	Wine	Comments

Date	Place And Occasion	Food	Wine	Comments

Still Life of Fruit on a Ledge Edward Ladell

Date	Place And Occasion	Food	Wine	Comments

Date	Place And Occasion	Food	Wine	Comments

DINNER PARTIES

Date	Guest List	Food	Wine	Comments

Date	Guest List	Food	Wine	Comments

Date	Guest List	Food	Wine	Comments

Date	Guest List	Food	Wine	Comments

NOTES OF TASTINGS

Date	Wine	Comments

The Wine Glass   Alonso Perez

Date	Wine	Comments

The Wine Festival Maurice Leloir

Date	Wine	Comments

Date	Wine	Comments

Date	Wine	Comments

Tom, Jerry and Logic Tasting Wine at London Docks Isaac Cruikshank

Date	Wine	Comments

Still Life of Fruit, a Bird's Nest and a Glass Edward Ladell

Contacts and Addresses

Name	Address	Telephone

Name	Address	Telephone

Name	Address	Telephone

Dinner at the Ambassadeurs   Jean Berand

Name	Address	Telephone

Name	Address	Telephone